AN ARTIST'S VIEW OF WORLD WAR II
DOG FACE

Chicken!

Das Henne!

written and illustrated
ROBERT C. KEM

I0624529

Soest, Germany, 7 April 1945

**To my children, grandchildren, and
the men of Company A, to whom I owe my life.**

DOG FACE

© 2014 Robert C. Kemp

Book Design by Bonnie JK Sheets.

ISBN 978-1892442-42-0 (pbk.: alk. paper)

02 03 04 05

www.dogfacewwii.com

Sgt. Robert C. Kemp

Mortar Squad Leader

2nd Platoon

Company A

58th Armored Infantry Battalion

8th Armored Division

9th U.S. Army

Foreword

This book is dedicated to the GIs—enemy and ally alike—who gave all they had, with very little or no recognition. Most were buried without ceremony, many in unmarked graves.

I felt for the new guys. We lost so many I got so I couldn't look them in the eye. Toward the end of the War, while we were mopping up in the Ruhr Valley, twelve recruits who hadn't been in Europe two days arrived on a halftrack. As they stopped, German artillery on the hill above us spotted them and started firing, "bracketing" them with .88 caliber shells. The first round hit short, and the boys jumped off the halftrack and started running. When the second round hit long, they stopped, and no matter how we yelled, they all ran back to shelter under the halftrack. That was the worst place to hide: not only were the Krauts zeroing in on them but a halftrack carries 1,000 pounds of explosives. The third round found the halftrack and we spent the next two hours trying to put bodies back together.

My graphics designer, editor, and daughter I never had says this story has no place in a comic book. Well, the word "funny" has many meanings, some of them not humorous at all. *That* kind of funny—the strange, inexplicable, and tragic—was everywhere in World War II. And sometimes it got so you had no tears left . . . you just laughed: it was *that* unbelievable and bizarre. And later, if you had any feelings left at all, you came apart. Nowadays they call it PTSD but we just called it "battle fatigue," as if a long nap could cure it. Not likely.

So, no, not every "comic" in this book is ha-ha funny. Some are heartbreaking and sad. But that's war, folks. Take it from a guy who was smack-dab in the middle of it.

Earlier, I dedicated the book to GIs, but I want to include a few lieutenants as well. I made friends with two: Bill Stockton, who got shot in both wrists while looking out a window. He was a platoon leader who later was elected as a Florida senator, and they named streets after him. The second was Lt. LaFrado, a sergeant who got a field commission and got shot in the leg an hour later.

After considering the many definitions of "funny," at the ripe old age of 90, the definition I like best is the one that makes people laugh and eases their pain. If there are a few tragic/funny moments in this little book, please bear with me. Life—and war—is a mixed bag and this book fits the bill. It made me laugh to write it . . . though I often broke down in tears remembering the fine men I knew then and miss now.

— *R Kamp*

Private! You will stand at attention at all times while I am surrendering!

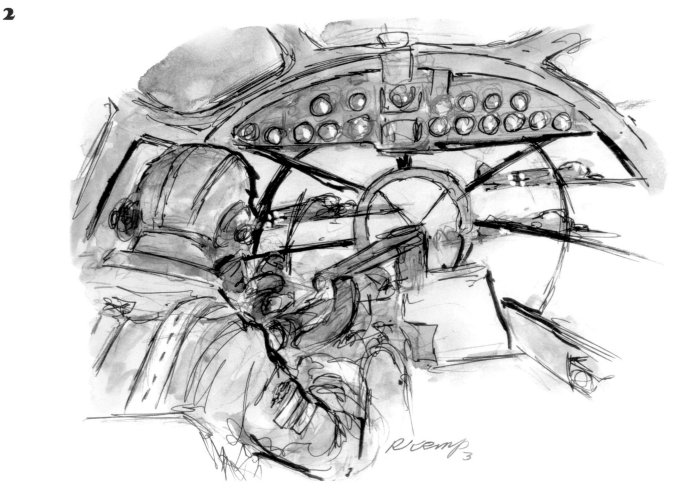

London Bridge is falling down, falling down!

Engaging a flight of Heinkel He-111 bombers, 1939. *-RK*

This is probably one of *your* stupid traps!

Private, Imperial Japanese Army. Warrant Officer, 77th Indian Brigade, Burma, 1943 -*RK*

I feel like a Christmas tree!

B-24J over Germany 1943. The gaudy paint jobs on the assembly ships
ensured that other bombers could find their proper squadron. -*RK*

Easy, mate! One of them might have a bottle of saki on him!

Here we go . . . all twisty, turny, willy nilly . . . there you are! *Got* ya, sucker!

Did you hear that?
Hear *what*? Go back to sleep!

Sgt. Hornsby, who hated my pal Lundy, told us to stay behind in a village to stop the two Tiger tanks headed our way. He insisted we fire on the Tigers from the upstairs house window with our two bazookas—which of course would have set the house on fire! He would then be rid of Lundy and me as well. The Tigers came and blew away half the house, but missed us completely, and when no one challenged them, they withdrew. *-RK*

Heil Hitler!

Sometimes, the front was in the rear. *-RK*

I wonder what's on the other side?

Please don't shoot me! I'm not SS!
My girlfriend thought it would be fun to go to a party dressed like this!

I didn't believe it, either. -RK

In the name of the Pilot and the Holy Navigator... please, parachute, I trust in thee!

The Airborne Prayer, on a Douglas DC Dakota, 1943. -RK

On patrol, Merretta found a piglet in the woods. He fed it some milk and settled in for the night. At about midnight, however, the 400 pound mother came looking for her baby. He and his bunk mate barely escaped with their lives. -RK

In basic training, we learned that placing a sleeping man's hand in a helmet full of warm water invariably makes him wet the bed. Doesn't seem funny now at all. *-RK*

I've got a luv-el-lee bunch of coak-y-nuts!

Or pineapples, depending on your unit.
4th Infantry Division, English Army. *-RK*

What? I was just saluting you, Sir!

Corporal, I don't think we are going to have a "political"
problem once we get this awful sweater off.

The last moment of Private Dumbjohn

After the war, I was at National Guard summer camp in San Diego, where I was asked to demonstrate bazookas. I placed several empty 50 gallon barrels out on the firing range, and shot ten rounds to show the men what the explosion was like. Two of the rounds didn't go off, so we set two guards to keep anyone from hurting themselves. The next morning we arrived to find the two guards dead—they had been playing catch with the unexploded rounds. -*RK*

Enough with the 'pitter-patter of the rain on the roof' stuff!

Sometimes, being trapped in a tent in a rainstorm with an optimist really got on your nerves. -*RK*

Let's not take a chance with this stupid grease gun . . .
We'd do better jumping out and scaring them to death!

Our M-1 machine gun was fine if the enemy was ten feet away. One time I fired at some
Germans across a small lake. The bullet splashed into the water halfway across.
When the attack was over, I disassembled it and threw it off the halftrack. *-RK*

Gertrude, I can't help it if the Colonel wants you for a while. I'll get you back, I promise!

Some men really got attached to their vehicles. If you messed
with a guy's jeep, it was like messing with his *wife. -RK*

Nasturtium?
Patagonia?

No matter how silly you felt saying it, if you didn't know the password, you were *dead*. -RK

Now, listen up, you new gyrenes! The first thing you've got to know is *who* you're supposed to take care of! *I'm* the who! Got it?

Easy on 'em, Sarge. They are still tender. *-RK*

Sorry, Sergeant, but we camouflaged the truck so well we can't find it!

Sorry it took me so long to get your cigarettes, Sarge. I traded that dry pair of socks you gave me for a chicken leg, which I traded for a candy bar. Then Sgt. Long gave me his extra pair of boots for the candy bar. Those boots got me a pack of Camels—which I know you don't like because they're non-filters—but the Camels bought me a brand-new canteen cup, which I traded for *two* Hershey bars! Then I traded one of the Hershey bars to some dumb private for—voila!—a pack of Marlboros, just like you asked for!

Bullets were flying everywhere and I cut my finger on a C-ration lid.

Even that lame excuse worked on the compassionate nurses. *-RK*

Hey, Lieutenant, do you ever feel like a sardine?

If you say the word *fireplace* one more time, Sergeant . . .

I was raised in Southern California. I never saw snow until I was twelve years—not days—old. We had a Swede in our unit that used to walk around in his undershirt in a blizzard. *-RK*

And a very Merry Christmas to you . . . anyway.

Well, lookie what Santy Claus done hung in our tree!

Doc, you gotta save these guys—they both owe me money!

Get 'em while they're hot!

The cooks would place a thermite cooker in a pan of water to heat the C-rations
until they were too hot to touch. We then had to wait until they were cold to eat them. *-RK*

They aren't going to paint one of those targets on *my* helmet!

When they gave LaFrado his field commission, they painted the bar
on the back of his helmet. He was wounded an hour later. *-RK*

What's so funny about putting an M-1 back together? Finding an extra part. *-RK*

**Whaddya mean,
ask him in *German?*
The bloke speaks better
English than *I* do!
He's been to *Oxford,*
ya blinkin' dink!**

I captured a German soldier who said he'd graduated from Oxford. He wore a heavy rucksack, which I offered to carry, but he declined. As I marched him to the stockade, he made fun of me to all the German civilians watching us from the windows of their homes. I put up with this until we arrived at the stockade, where I shoved him through the gate and yanked the rucksack off his back. Inside were a hundred boxes of "Chocacola" candy bars, each three inches in diameter. It was my only act of looting during the war. *-RK*

I see you have been reducing the rations again, Sergeant.

I don't remember there not being enough, but the quality needed some work. -RK

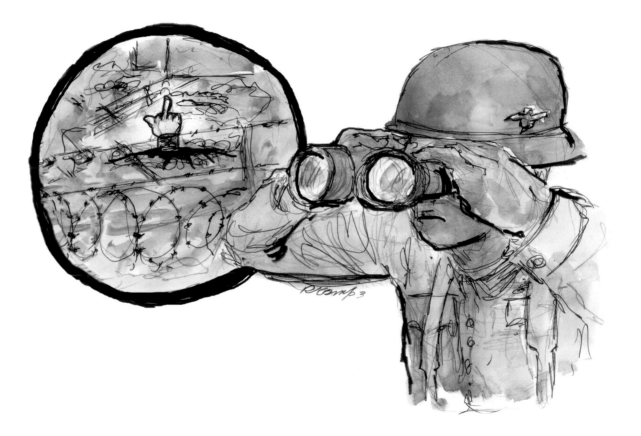

Vas is mit mittle fenger, hmm?

3rd German Air Force Infantry, Ruhr Valley, 1944. -*RK*

If I catch your men sipping tea before 4 o'clock, none of you will get guard duty for a blinkin' month!

As opposed to American GIs, Gurkhas *loved* guard duty.
Corporal of the 9th Gurkha Rifles and a British Captain, Grenadier, on loan to the Indian Army. *-RK*

**Come *on*, Captain! You *always* get to drive! I *never, ever* get to drive!
Damn it, Captain! *Lemme have that stick*! I'll show 'em!**

Sounds like my 16 year-old grandson. A B-24 Liberator over Germany, 1944. *-RK*

Stick out your tongue and say *ahh*.

Everyone was afraid of our nearsighted medic. *-RK*

. . . riding high, *under* the sun. Whew.

Uh, Sergeant . . . I think that last road sentry was German.

That's just a pea-shooter. Now, *this* is a real gun!

Italian soldier with his Beretta and an American GI with his MG-34 machine gun. *-RK*

Welcome to the blinkin' chicken coup! Let's go lay some *eggs!*

Lancaster Bomber, 57th Squadron, East Kirby, Lincolnshire, England. *-RK*

Anatomy of a cadet

When you first arrived at the Cadet Training Center, you hated the endless discipline.
Gradually, however, you began to like it and couldn't get enough. Sick, huh? -RK

B-24J Liberator bomber out of Bolsover, England, 1943.

Great: I'm warm and I'm checked out on targets . . . but now I can't *move*.

8th Air Force, England, 1944. Fitted with all the gear to keep you alive, you couldn't fit in the cockpit. *-RK*

I had a nice job as a cook's helper, then some smart ass said something about the Air Cadets!

Okay. Alright. Some of our guys are chicken.

No disrespect intended, Sir, but how in the hell did you get yourself into this mess?

Somewhere in the Rhur Valley, 1945. *-RK*

I can't make up my mind. Flowers or fruit?

A new nurse Lieutenant gets her first steel helmet. -*RK*

No matter how ugly, dumb, or lazy you were,
there was someone at home who worshiped the ground you walked on.

Merretta, leave those darn apples alone and tend to business!

After a while, patrol got so boring you started doing strange things. -RK

Komen out! Ve know you are in dere!

(Give 'em a couple more seconds thinking they got us . . . then we'll get *them*.)

If I put my head down any lower, Captain, I'll be lookin' outta my *you-know-what*.

1945. Just another day in the Ruhr Valley cleaning up Patton's mess. -*RK*

I'm too scared to move . . . but there's a thermite grenade in my belt . . .

We opened the doors two inches and came nose-to-nose with a Panther tank.
Lundy slid a grenade down the barrel and we ran like hell! *-RK*

You're busted in rank, Private, so it looks like we'll be taking that arm off.

It's always a bad idea to make permanent that which is temporary. -RK

Merrily, we roll along!

M-3 halftrack with three .30 caliber machine guns, a rack of 20 land mines—that's a half ton of explosives—, a driver, an NCO squad leader, six PFCs, and a medic. *-RK*

Hero, my ass!
I'll be a *dead* hero!
All *he* wants is to fill up his two-fer with our dog tags!

I was leader of a mortar squad in the Ruhr Valley in 1944. We cleaned up behind the 2nd Armored Division, who shot ahead, trapping a huge chunk of the German Army. It was left to us to take care of the boxed-in enemy while all Patton had to worry about was gasoline for moving forward. -RK

You mean *this* is the entire South African Air Force?

Lieutenant, British Royal Air Force, South Africa. *-RK*

Mother says, "Don't worry, the action has moved to another sector, and we have 'em on the *run*"!

Folks at home were sometimes led astray by reporters
who were reporting action from a position far behind the front. *-RK*

Those guys never drive under thirty miles an hour!

Food delivery trucks didn't want to stay at the front any longer than absolutely necessary. -RK

Baseball, yah. But *hot* hund?

A German soldier finds a letter addressed to an American GI, telling of
taking a nephew to a baseball game and buying him a hot dog. -*RK*

Star light, star bright, first star I see tonight . . .

No radio beacons out here—your navigator better know his stuff.
Navigator, B-24 bomber over Germany, 1944. *-RK*

All the Germans had to do was to poison their delicious
bottled white cherries and they would have won the war. -*RK*

Never mind the incoming fire! Get those new 10-in-1 rations with bacon off the tank before our guys *inside* start shooting at us!

One 48-ton Patton tank, one 90mm gun, one .130 caliber machine gun, one .50 caliber machine gun, and five really pissed-off tankers. -*RK*

You think *this* one is big, you
should see the one that *got* away!

I forget, is it potatoes, then soup, then spinach, then lime Jello . . . or is it . . . ?

When we got into combat, it wasn't their fault we lost our mess kits and had to eat
everything thrown together into our canteen cups. My grandfather used to say,
"After the food passes your tongue, your stomach doesn't care what it looked like." We survived. -RK

Don't shoot till he's out of the water—I really need a *bath*!

You had to take advantage of every opportunity. When we got to Epley, France, there was four feet of snow on the ground and everything was frozen. Our squad was assigned a cheese factory as a billet. There was a big, broken cooking pot we used as a bathtub, which worked great in the fireplace, except the chimney was plugged and smoke went everywhere. Burning a creosote telephone pole as firewood didn't help either. -RK

*I am behind enemy lines. I am hungry. I'm sick of Hitler and the War.
I want to go home to my wife and kids. I need to learn American!
Yankee Doodle Dandy, put a noodle in my hair, and sing it . . .*

Last check, sir: life jacket, boots, teddy bear—in case you get shot down over enemy territory, you'll have something to hang on to—goggles, helmet, gloves, candy bars, gum . . .

Your mechanic had a huge responsibility. If he wasn't good, your chances of surviving were nill. -RK

Damn! *One* dent in a canteen cup and it won't fit over the canteen!

Next to your rifle, your canteen cup was the most important piece of equipment you owned. We'd drink out of it, eat out of it, urinate in it when we were pinned down, and use it to dig with. It was easy to clean: we'd fill it with water, then drop in a capsule of C-ration lemonade. The citric acid ate away the aluminum and it shined like new. And no, we didn't drink the lemonade. *-RK*

**Hi, sweetie!
Want a bite of my Hershey bar?**

The nearsighted PFC on his first leave
to London will probably live after the
Scot soldier gets done with him, but
he will be more careful next time. *-RK*

Now, make like a cross on a church!

This was the punishment for a serious blunder.
Sgt. Hudson always managed to make his point absolutely clear to his troops. *-RK*

Charlie says everything is fine, and he is somewhere called . . . um . . . uh . . .

Charlie should have known you never tell your unit's location. After you wrote a letter, you left it unsealed and gave it to the platoon sergeant and he in turn gave it to the platoon leader who crossed out everything he thought would be of interest to the enemy with a big black marker. It was called censoring. -RK

You didn't really cook that in your helmet, did you?
I would have cooked it in *your* helmet, but it had a hole in it.

Cooking in your steel helmet was common. We all had little gas stoves, but the meat always tasted of paint. -RK

Out of gas? Poor baby! Want a ride to the stockade?

We found one German tank pulling two others, because we had cut off their gasoline supply. -*RK*

Make sure the General isn't around when you decide to try on his hat. -*RK*

Ringing the bell

When the steel helmet first came out, not everyone knew to anchor it with a helmet liner, so they were loose on a lot of guys. Here Sgt. Hudson is testing for liner and helmet attachments. -*RK*

Sarge, tell me there ain't *really* any werewolves up in those hills.

After Germany's surrender, a bunch of die-hard SS troops escaped to the Hartz mountains to run guerilla operations. In nearby villages, they posted notices about werewolves in the forest to scare the people—and us. One day a boy told us that a German sergeant insulted his sister and he knew where they were hiding. We found the whole bunch of them in an underground bunker we had walked over ten times! *-RK*

**Gripe, gripe, gripe! They get *one* hot meal a week, rain or shine.
What *more* do they want?**

It must have been hard to get something edible *and* hot to the front lines.
You weren't sure where you were headed. We weren't sure where we were, either.
Come to think of it, how we ever got anything hot to eat was a *miracle.* -RK

**I say, Nigel, go ahead and give the bloke a cup of tea,
but remember, when we get him to the stockade, *I get his boots!***

Wearing boots like that wouldn't be out of uniform for anyone in this outfit. -*RK*

Achtung! Stay away from ze plane mit der "K" on der tail—it's a trap!

B-17J, over Germany, 1945. In the distance are FW-190 Ramjaggers,
whose pilots took an oath to either shoot down a bomber or ram it and parachute to safety.
We, too, had our tactics for confusing the enemy. -RK

Well now, dis here thingy is called a Nut Twister.
Later, I'll tell you about the Screw Twister, and then the Nuckle Buster!

It was important that those engines run like a Swiss watch, so they had
only the most *qualified* personnel filling those positions. -RK

The Jerry Can sure adds to the bouquet!

On VE day, we liberated a Schnaaps distillery and filled fifty gasoline cans with fermented "freedom." -RK

Tiptoe through the tulips . . .

Step on a land mine, you disappeared. Step on a shoe mine, you lost a foot.
Step on a Bouncing Betty, you got a change of voice. *-RK*

A message from headquarters.

The Mark IV tank used by the British during WWI had two six
pound cannons, two Lewis machine guns . . . and a nest of pigeons. *-RK*

Demotion ... #1 ... #2 ... #3.

Getting a reduction in rank was not only humiliating, it meant a lot less money to lose at poker. *-RK*

Don't tell me to go to hell, Sergeant. I just *came* from there!

Has anyone seen that bowl of ground up chicken guts I fixed for the dog?

Well now, aren't you a fancy one? Wouldn't my sainted mama love to see *you*?

Corporal, VI Eritrea Battalion, Italian Army, meets our T-5 truck driver. If it hadn't been for these guys, we would have froze, starved, and had to beat the enemy with empty rifles. -*RK*

When the Admiral's home, you think his wife makes *him* do the dishes?

That's a 27-ton Cromwell tank. Maybe they just stopped for tea . . .

After the Bulge, we advanced so fast sometimes the line you
fell back to became the rest area for the other side. -RK

We're gonna have a clean sweep to and fro, catch those corners as you go!

Days consisted of reveille, breakfast, sweep, sweep, sweep, lunch, sweep some more, then dinner. *-RK*

Row, row, row your boat, gently away from submarines . . .

It took us fourteen days to sail from New York to England. We were chased into the Bay of Biscay by German submarines, called "Wolfpacks." I didn't worry, but I *did* spend a lot of time on deck. *-RK*

This is how it happened!   Nein, *nein*!"

A P-51 Mustang pilot and a Focke-Wulf 190 Butcher Bird pilot share different versions of the same dogfight. -RK

Well, maybe some beautiful French girl will claim them!

GIs—American or German—all think the same. -*RK*

I know they're surrendering, Lieutenant, but just look at all those *rifles!*

Toward the end of the war, the 8th Division was stopped on our way to Berlin. Suddenly
we saw a whole army of surrendering troops marching by, and I thought, *Wow! What a sight! -RK*